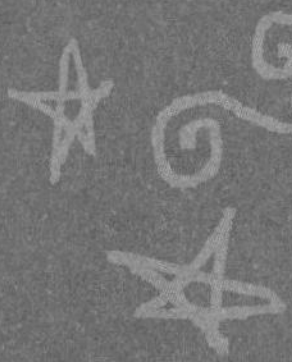

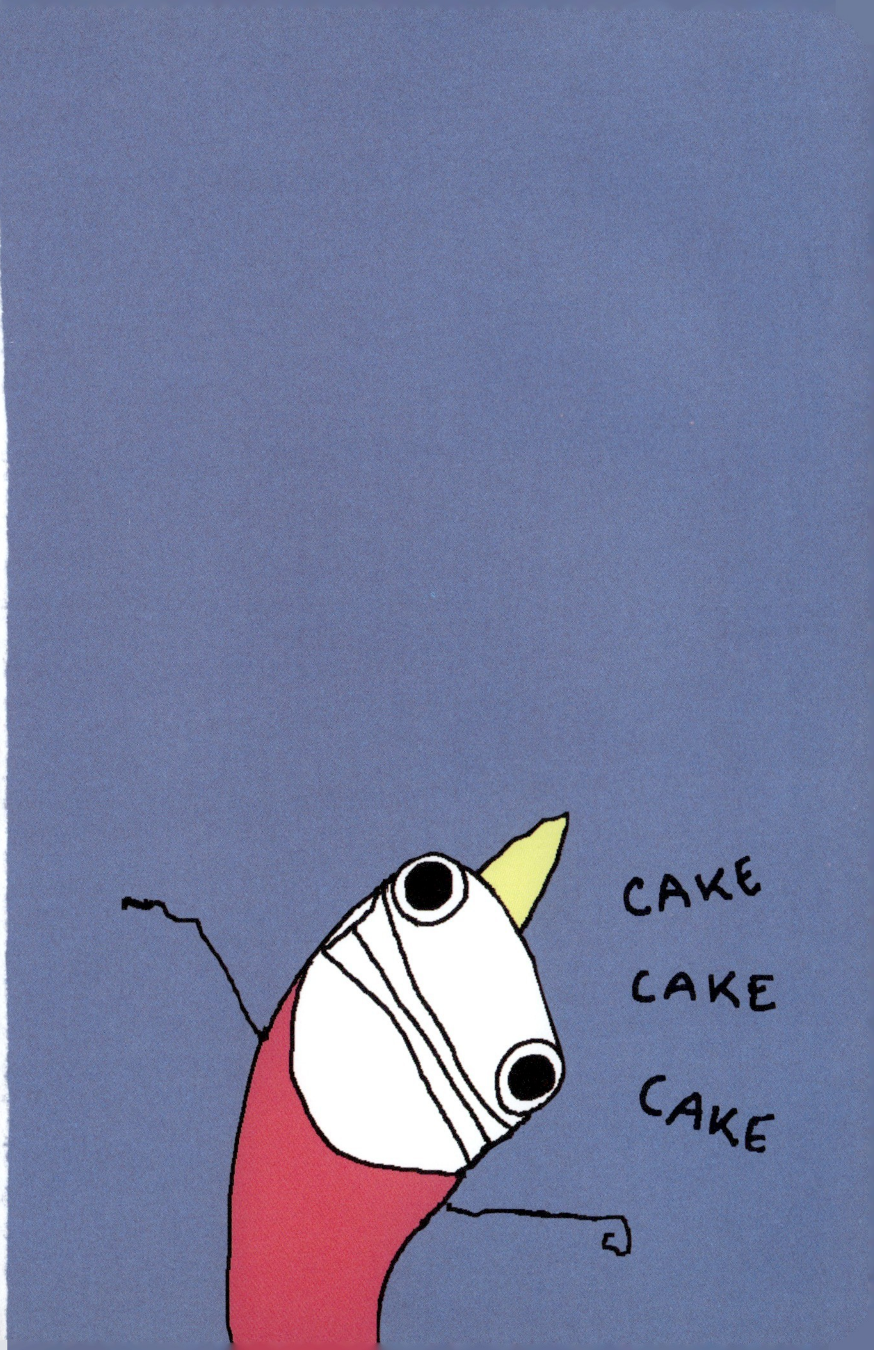
CAKE
CAKE
CAKE

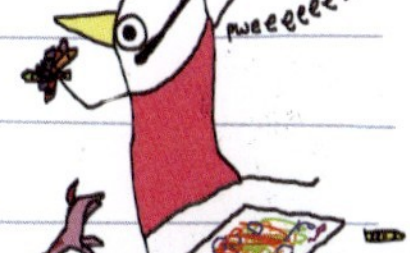
wheeeeee.....

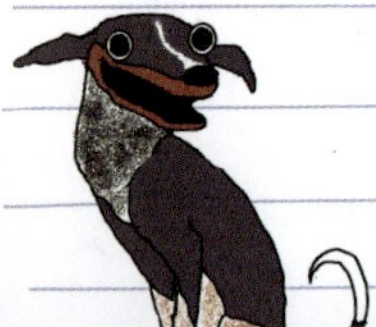

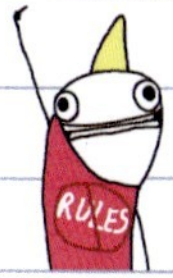
RULES

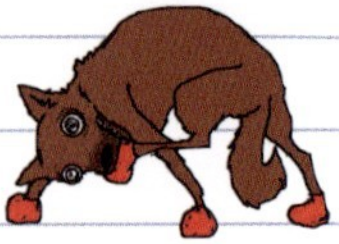

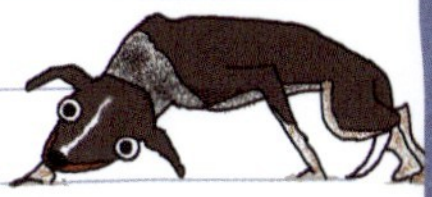

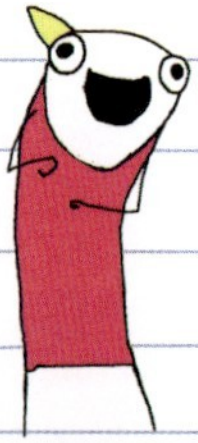

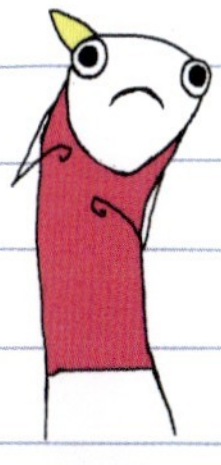

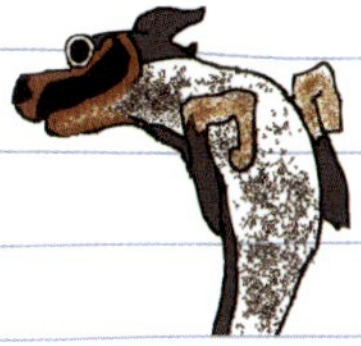

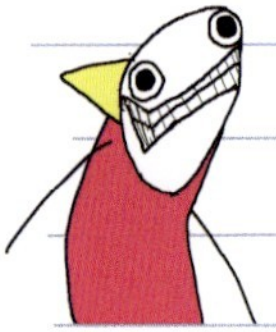

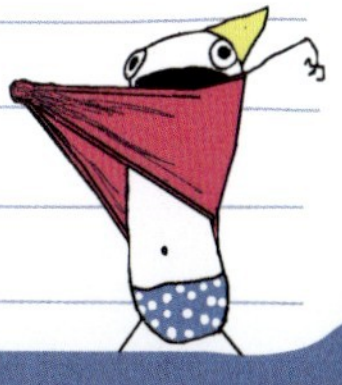

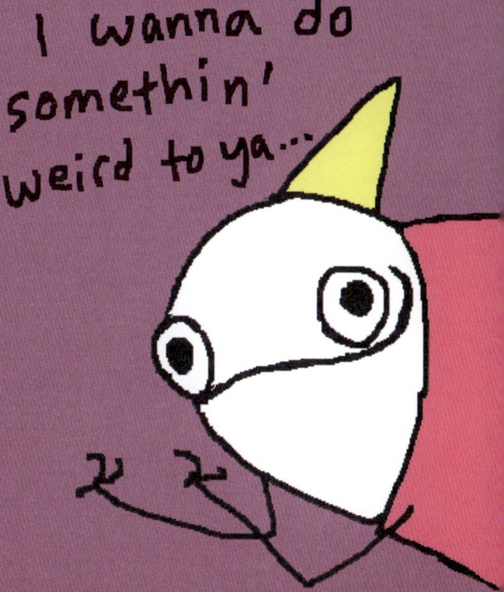
I wanna do somethin' weird to ya...

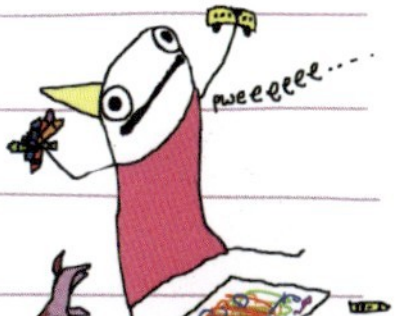
pweeeeee....

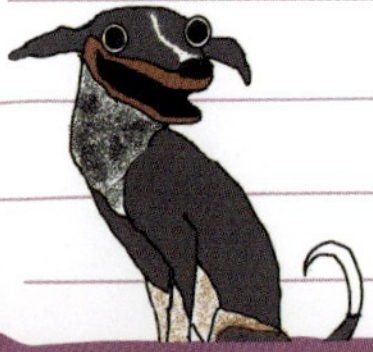

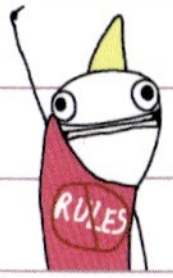
RULES

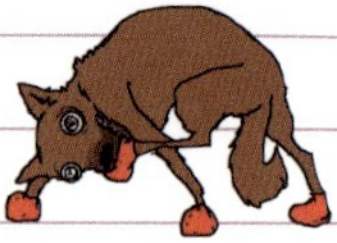

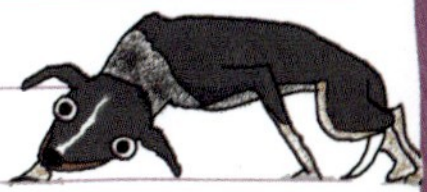

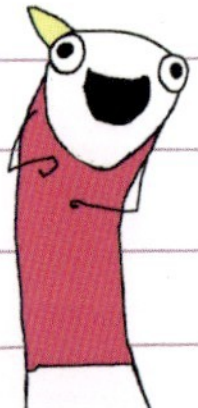

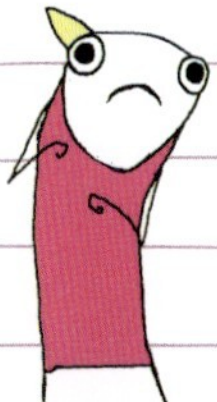

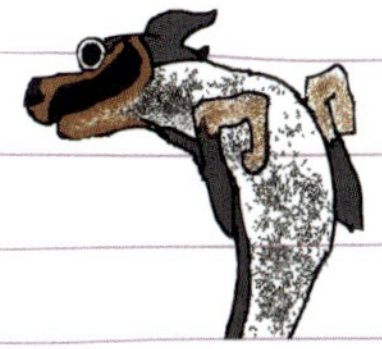

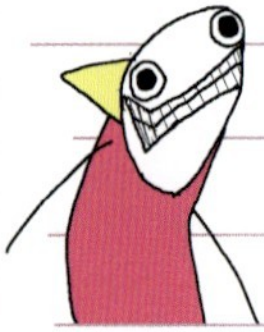

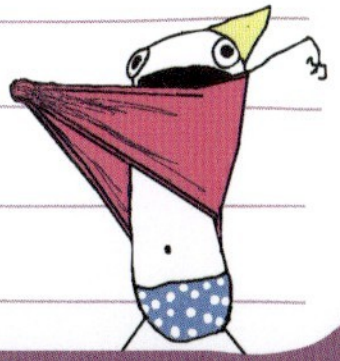

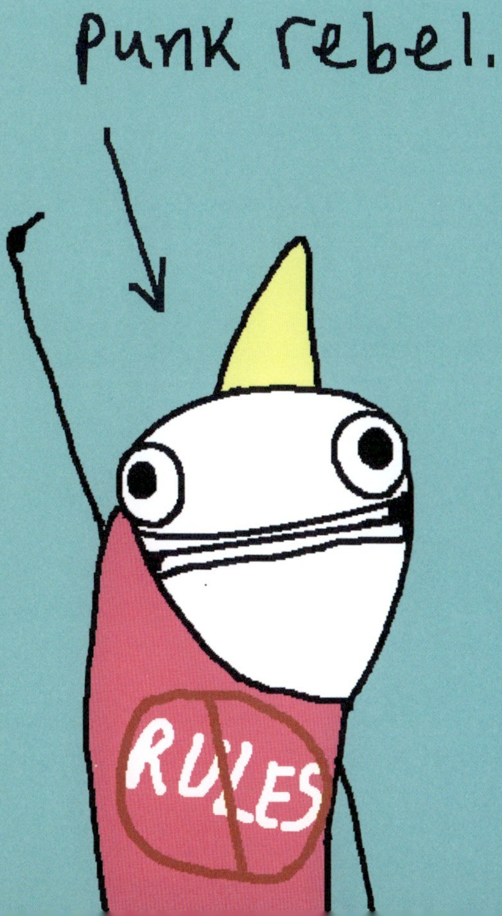
punk rebel.
RULES

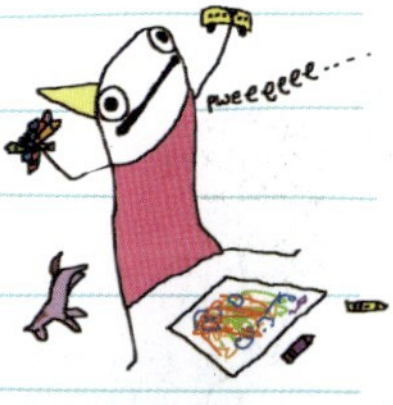
pweeeeee....

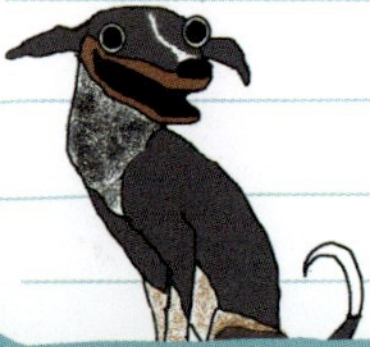

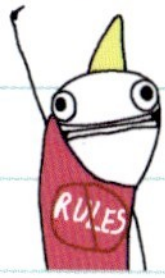
RULES

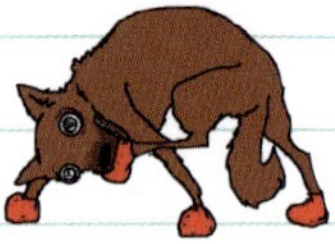

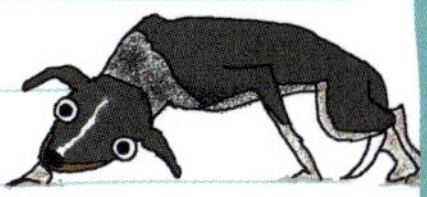

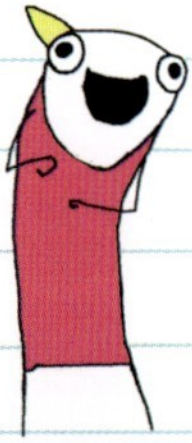

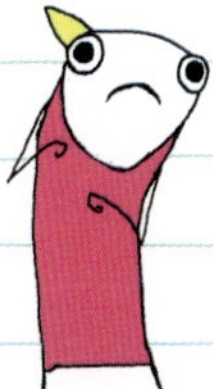

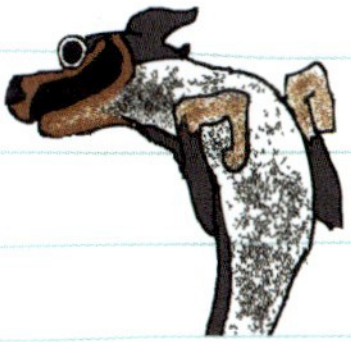

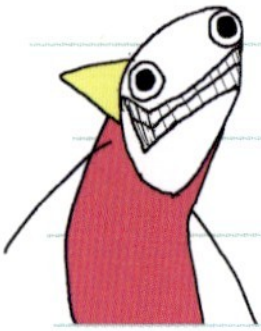

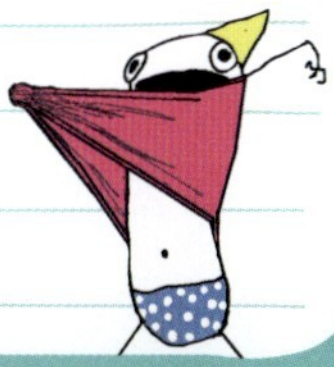

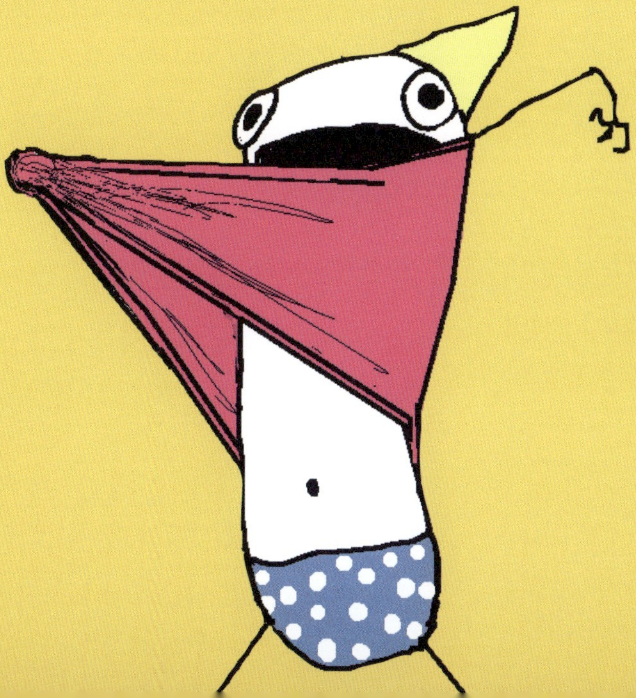

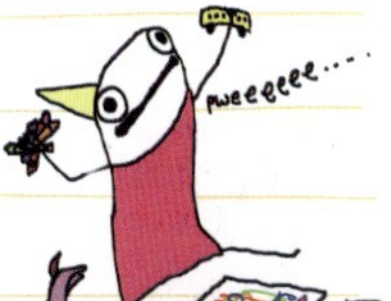

Pweeeeee....

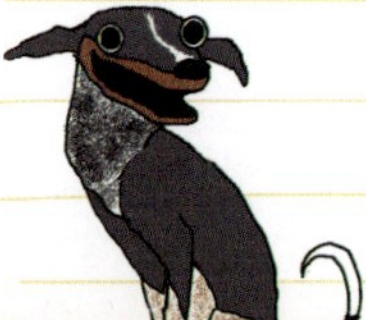

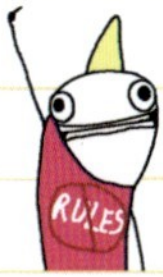
RULES

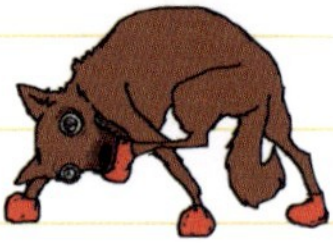

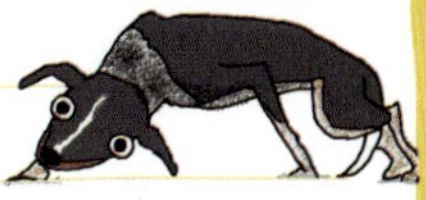

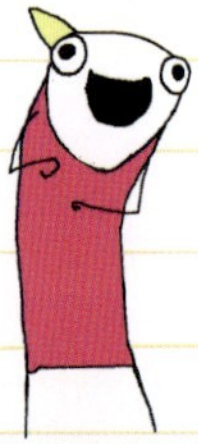

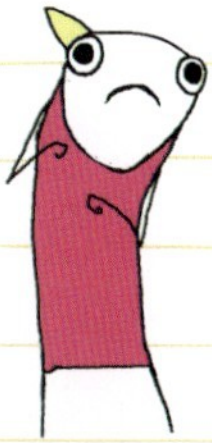

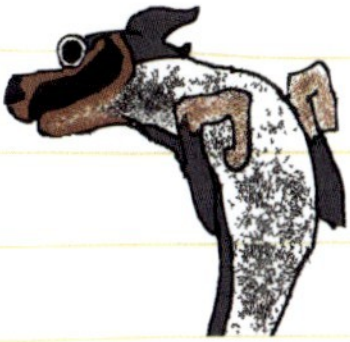

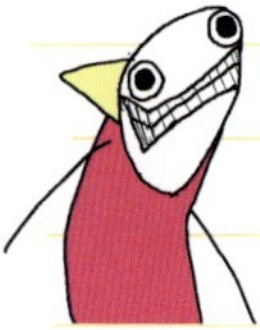

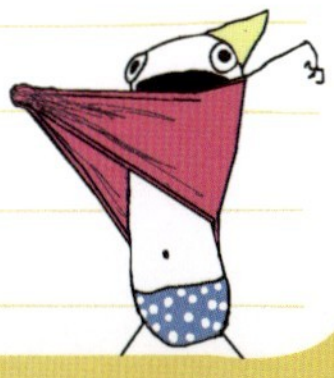

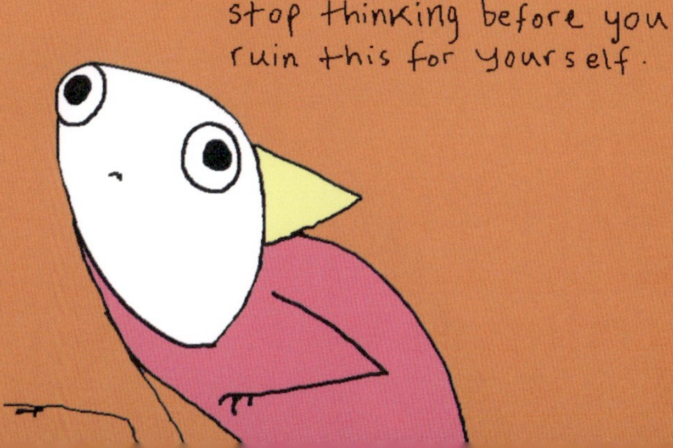
stop thinking before you ruin this for yourself.

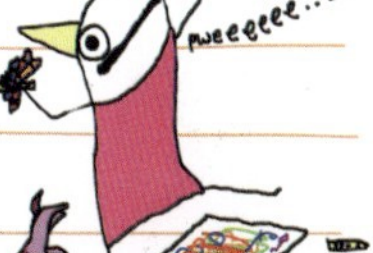
Pweeeeee.....

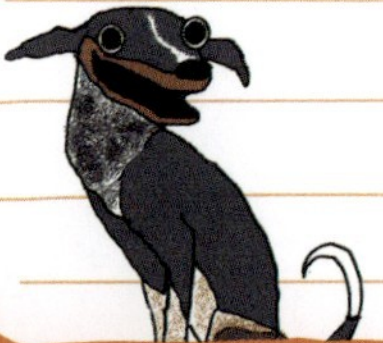

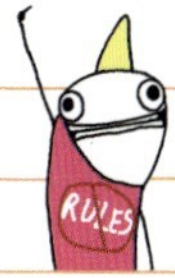
RULES

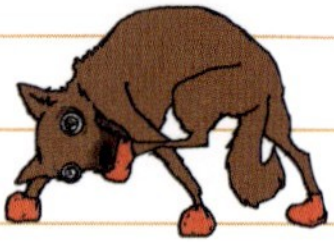

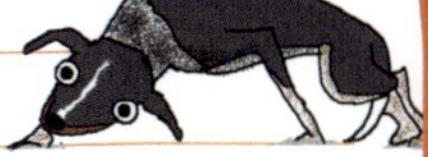

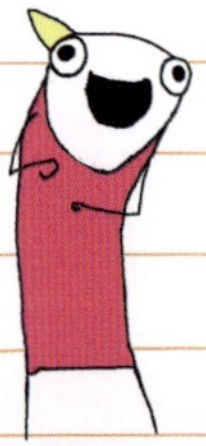

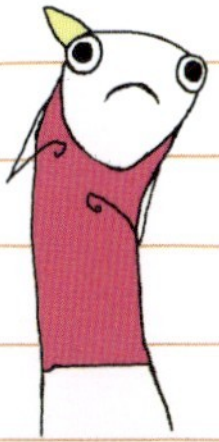

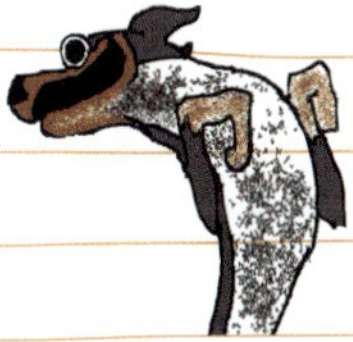

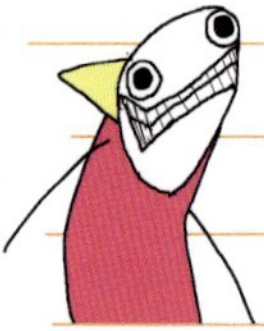

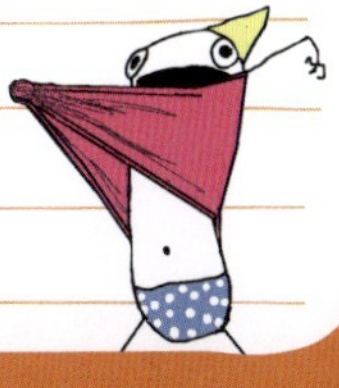